Céline Marie Claudette **Dion** CC OQ ChLD, born on 30th March 1968, Charlemagne, Quebec, Canada is a singer. Born into a large family Céline emerged as a teen star in her homeland with a series of French-language albums during the 1980s. She first received international recognition by winning the Yamaha World Popular Song Festival 1982 then the Eurovision Song Contest of 1988, where she represented Switzerland. After learning to speak English, Dion signed to Epic Records in the US, releasing her debut English-language L.P., Unison in 1990, establishing herself as a pop artist in North America and other English-speaking areas of the world.

Céline became famous worldwide during the 1990s, after issuing several best-selling English albums including Falling into You (1996) then Let's Talk About Love (1997), both of which were certified diamond in the US. She also had a series of international chart-toppers, including "The Power of Love", "Think Twice", "Because You Loved Me", "It's All Coming Back to Me Now", "My Heart Will Go On", and "I'm Your Angel".

Dion continued releasing French L.Ps between each English record, D'eux (1995) becoming the best-selling French-language album of all time, while S'il suffisait d'aimer (1998), Sans attendre (2012), and Encore un soir (2016) were all certified diamond in France. Céline built her reputation as a highly successful live performer during the 2000s with A New Day... in Las Vegas Strip (2003–07), which remains the highest-grossing concert residency of all time, followed by the Taking Chances World Tour (2008–09), one of the highest-grossing concert tours of all time.

Dion's music has been influenced by genres ranging from rock and R&B to gospel and classical, her recordings mainly being in

French and English, although she has also sung in Spanish, Italian, German, Latin, Japanese, and Mandarin Chinese. While her issues have frequently attracted a mixed critical reception, she is regarded as one of pop music's most influential voices.

Céline has won 5 Grammy Awards, including Album of the Year and Record of the Year. Billboard named her the "Queen of Adult Contemporary" for having the most chart-toppers on the radio format for a female artist. She is the 2nd best-selling female artist in the US during the Nielsen SoundScan era. Dion was honoured by the International Federation of the Phonographic Industry (IFPI) during 2003, for selling over 50 million L.Ps in Europe. She is the best-selling Canadian artist ever, with record sales of over 200 million copies worldwide.

Céline was born in Charlemagne, Quebec, 15 miles northeast of Montreal, the youngest of 14 children of Thérèse (née Tanguay), a housewife, and Adhémar Dion, a butcher, both of French-Canadian descent. She was raised a Roman Catholic, in a poor but happy home in Charlemagne. Music had always been a big part of life for the Dion family, so she was named after the song "Céline", which French singer Hugues Aufray had recorded two years before her birth.

At the age of 5, Céline made her first public appearance at her brother Michel's wedding, on 13th August 1973, when she sang Christine Charbonneau's song "Du fil des aiguilles et du coton". Dion continued to perform with her siblings in her parents' small piano bar called Le Vieux Baril, "The Old Barrel", having dreamt of being a performer from an early age. In an interview with People magazine in 1994, she recalled, "I missed my family and my home, but I don't regret having lost my adolescence. I had one dream: I wanted to be a singer."

Céline collaborated with her mother and her brother Jacques when aged 12, to write and compose her first song, "Ce n'était qu'un rêve", ("It Was Only a Dream" or "Nothing But A Dream"). Her brother Michel sent the recording to music manager René Angélil, whose name he discovered on the back of a Ginette Reno album. Angélil was moved to tears by Dion's voice, so decided to make her a star.

René mortgaged his home to fund her first record, La voix du bon Dieu, which later became a local No. 1 hit, making her a star in Quebec. Céline's popularity spread to other parts of the world when she competed in the Yamaha World Popular Song Festival in Tokyo, Japan, in 1982, winning the musician's award for "Top Performer," as well as the gold medal for "Best Song," with "Tellement j'ai d'amour pour toi".

As well as becoming the first Canadian artist to receive a gold record in France during 1983, for the single "D'amour ou d'amitié" ("Of Love or of Friendship"), Dion also won several Félix Awards, including "Best Female performer" and "Discovery of the Year". More success came when Céline represented Switzerland in the Eurovision Song Contest of 1988, with the song "Ne partez pas sans moi," winning a close contest in Dublin, Ireland.

Following seeing a Michael Jackson performance at the age of 18, Dion told Angélil that she wanted to be a star like Jackson. Though confident in her talent, René realized that her image needed to be changed for her to be marketed worldwide. Celine stayed out of the spotlight for a number of months, during which she underwent dental surgery to improve her appearance, being sent to the École Berlitz during 1989 to polish her English. During a concert on the Incognito tournée that year she injured her vocal cords, so consulted the otorhinolaryngologist William Gould, who told her to either have surgery or not to use them at all for 3 weeks. Dion chose the latter then underwent vocal training with William Riley.

Two years after she learned English, Celine made her debut into the Anglophone market with Unison (1990), the lead single having originally been recorded by Laura Branigan. She received the help of many established musicians, including Vito Luprano and Canadian producer David Foster. The L.P. was mainly influenced by soft rock music of the 1980s, soon finding a niche within the adult contemporary radio format.

Unison impressed the critics: Jim Faber of Entertainment Weekly having written that Dion's vocals were "tastefully unadorned", and that she never attempted to "bring off styles that are beyond her". Stephen Erlewine of AllMusic declared that it was "a fine, sophisticated American debut". Singles from the album included "(If There Was) Any Other Way", "The Last to Know", "Unison", and "Where Does My Heart Beat Now", a mid-tempo soft-rock ballad, with electric guitar to the fore, whch became Celine's first top-10 hit on the US Billboard Hot 100, making # 4. She was a featured soloist on Voices That Care during 1991, a tribute to US troops fighting in Operation Desert Storm.

Dion's real international breakthrough came when she duetted with Peabo Bryson on the title track to Disney's animated movie Beauty and the Beast (1991), which became her first top-10 entry in the UK then her 2nd US top-10 hit. Its songwriters won an Academy Award for Best Song, while Celine received her first Grammy Award for Best Pop Performance by a Duo or Group with Vocal.

"Beauty and the Beast" was the lead single from her eponymous L.P. in 1992, which like her debut, had a strong pop rock influence, combined with elements of soul and classical music. Helped by the success of its lead-off single and her collaborations with David Foster and Diane Warren, the album sold even better than Unison, being certified diamond in Canada then double platinum in the US. The L.P's 2nd single "If You Asked Me To", a cover of Patti LaBelle's song from the movie Licence to Kill (1989), became her first chart-topping single in Canada, having hit # 4 on the US Billboard Hot 100.

Dion then issued the Francophone album Dion chante Plamondon, comprised mainly of covers, but featuring 4 new songs: "Des mots qui sonnent", "Je danse dans ma tête", "Quelqu'un que j'aime, quelqu'un qui m'aime" and "L'amour existe encore". It was first released in Canada and France during the 1991–1992 period, being certified Gold the day it was put out in Quebec, before becoming the first French Celine Dion L.P. to be issued internationally in 1994. "Un garçon pas comme les autres (Ziggy)" became a big hit in France, making No. 2, later being certified gold.

Her L.Ps Unison and Céline Dion, together with many high-profile media appearances had propelled Dion to superstardom in North America by 1992, having achieved one of her main objectives. However, her French fans in Canada criticized her for neglecting them, in response to which, at the 1991 Félix Awards show, after winning "English Artist of the Year", Céline refused to accept the award, having said that she was—and would always be—a French, not an English, artist. As well as her commercial success, there were also changes in Dion's personal life, as her manager Angélil, who was 26 years her senior, became her lover. However, their relationship was kept secret, as both were concerned that the public would regard it as inappropriate.

Céline announced her feelings for her manager during 1993, declaring him "the colour of love" in the dedication section of her third English-language album The Colour of My Love. However, instead of criticizing their relationship as she'd feared, fans embraced the couple. Angélil and Dion then married in an extravagant wedding ceremony in December of the following year, which was broadcast live on Canadian TV.

As with most of Celine's records, The Colour of my Love had themes of love and romance, becoming her greatest success so far, selling more than 6 million copies in the US, with 2 million in Canada, while topping the charts in many other countries. The L.P. also produced Dion's first US, Canadian, and Australian No. 1 single "The Power of Love", a remake of Jennifer Rush's 1985 hit, which became her signature hit until her career reached new heights during the late 1990s.

The single "When I Fall in Love", a duet with Clive Griffin, had some success on the US and Canadian charts, being nominated for two Grammy Awards, winning one. The Colour of My Love also became Celine's first major hit in Europe, especially in the UK, where both the album and the single, "Think Twice," topped the British charts for 5 successive weeks simultaneously. "Think Twice", which stayed at No. 1 for 7 weeks, became the 4th single by a female artist to sell over a million copies in the UK, while the L.P. was certified 5-times platinum for two million copies sold.

Dion remained true to her French roots, having continued to issue many Francophone recordings between each English record, which were mainly received better than her English-language discs. Celine released À l'Olympia, a live album that was recorded during one of her concerts at the Paris Olympia in 1994, with one promotional single, a live version of "Calling You", which made # 75 on the French Singles Chart.

Dion also recorded a bilingual version of Petit Papa Noël with Alvin and the Chipmunks for the festive L.P., A Very Merry Chipmunk in 1994. D'eux, also known as The French Album in the US, was released during the following year, which went on to become the best-selling French-language L.P. of all time.

The record was largely written and produced by Jean-Jacques Goldman, having great success with the singles "Pour que tu m'aimes encore" and "Je sais pas", the former topping the French charts for 12 weeks, later being certified Platinum in France. The single reached the top 10 in the UK and Ireland, a rare achievement for a French song. The 2nd single off the album, "Je sais pas", also topped the French Singles Chart, going Silver there. The songs later became "If That's What It Takes" and "I Don't Know" on her next English L.P., Falling into You.

From the mid-1990s Celine's albums were usually mainly melodramatic soft rock ballads, having sprinklings of up-tempo pop with rare forays into other genres. She collaborated with many renowned writers and producers, including Jim Steinman and David Foster, who helped her to develop a signature sound.

While critical reviews varied, her issues performed increasingly well on the international charts, having established herself as one of the best-selling artists in the world by the mid-1990s. Dion won the World Music Award for "World's Best-selling Female Recording Artist of the Year" for the third time during 1996.

Falling into You (1996), Celine's 4th English-language L.P., was released at the height of her popularity, having shown a further progression in her music. Dion tried to reach a wider audience, combining many elements, including complex orchestral sounds, African chanting, and elaborate musical effects, using the violin, Spanish guitar, trombone, cavaquinho, and saxophone among others to create a new sound.

The album produced singles taking in a variety of musical styles. The title track "Falling into You", with the Tina Turner cover" River Deep – Mountain High", made prominent use of percussion instruments, while "It's All Coming Back to Me Now", produced by its writer Jim Steinman, and a remake of Eric Carmen's "All by Myself," maintained a soft-rock atmosphere, combined with the classical sound of the piano. The chart-topping single "Because You Loved Me", written by Diane Warren, was a pop ballad that was used as the theme to the film Up Close and Personal (1996).

Overall, Falling into You received career-best reviews for Celine, although Dan Leroy wrote that it wasn't very different from her previous work, with Stephen Holden of The New York Times and Natalie Nichols of the Los Angeles Times stating that the album was formulaic. However, other critics, including Chuck Eddy of Entertainment Weekly, Stephen Thomas Erlewine of AMG, and

Daniel Durchholz, described the L.P. as "compelling", "passionate", "stylish", "elegant", and "remarkably well-crafted". Falling Into You was Dion's biggest selling album, topping the charts in many countries, becoming one of the best-selling L.Ps of all time.

CBC Music ranked Falling into you at 33rd on their list of the 100 greatest Canadian albums ever during 2013. In the US, the L.P. topped the charts, later being certified 11× Platinum for over 11 million copies shipped. In Canada, the album was certified diamond for over one million copies shipped. The IFPI certified Falling into You as 9× Platinum, being one of only 3 L.Ps in history to reach that sales threshold, with one of the other two being Dion's own album, Let's Talk About Love. The record also won Grammy Awards for Best Pop Album and the academy's highest honour Album of the Year.

Celine was invited to sing "The Power of the Dream" at the opening ceremony of the Atlanta Olympic Games during the summer of 1996, having launched the Falling into You Tour in support of her new L.P. that March, performing in concerts around the world for over a year. Dion followed Falling into You with Let's Talk About Love (1997), which was promoted as its sequel.

The album was recorded in London, New York City, and Los Angeles, featuring a host of guests, including Barbra Streisand on "Tell Him"; the Bee Gees on "Immortality"; and tenor Luciano Pavarotti on "I Hate You Then I Love You". Other musicians included Carole King, Sir George Martin, Bryan Adams and Jamaican singer Diana King, who added a reggae tinge to "Treat Her Like a Lady".

Let's Talk About Love was another great success, topping the charts all over the world, going platinum in 24. countries, becoming the fastest selling L.P. of her career. The album topped the the US chart in its 7th week of issue, later being certified 10× Platinum in the States for over 10 million copies shipped. The L.P. sold 230,212 copies in its first week of release in Canada, which is still a record, later being certified diamond for over 1 million shipped. The most successful single from the album was the classically influenced ballad "My Heart Will Go On", written and composed by James Horner and Will Jennings, produced by Horner and Walter Afanasieff.

Used as the love theme for the box office hit movie Titanic (1997), the song topped the charts across the world, becoming Celine's signature song. Horner and Jennings won the Academy Award and Golden Globe for Best Original Song, while Dion received two Grammy Awards for "Best Female Pop Vocal Performance" and "Record of the Year". "My Heart Will Go On" and "Think Twice" made Celine the only female artist in the UK to have had two singles selling over a million copies. In support of her L.P., she went on the Let's Talk About Love Tour from 1998 - 1999.

Dion ended the 20th century with 3 more hit albums: the Christmas L.P. These Are Special Times (1998), the French-language album, S'il suffisait d'aimer, and the compilation L.P. All the Way... A Decade of Song (1999). On the first of these, she co-wrote the song "Don't Save It All For Christmas Day" along with Ric Wake and Peter Zizzo. The album was her most classically influenced yet, with orchestral arrangements on almost every track.

The L.P. featured the single "I'm Your Angel", a duet with R. Kelly, which became Celine's 4th single to top the US charts, becoming a big hit worldwide. The album's 2nd single "The Prayer", a duet with Andrea Bocelli, was on the soundtrack of the film Quest for Camelot (1998), having won a Golden Globe Award for Best Original Song. All the Way... A Decade of Song, brought together her most successful hits, together with 7 new songs, including the lead-off single "That's the Way It Is", a cover of Roberta Flack's "The First Time Ever I Saw Your Face", and "All the Way", a duet with Frank Sinatra.

All the Way became one of the best-selling compilation L.Ps of all time, topping the US charts for 3 weeks, later being certified 7x Platinum in the States for 7 million copies shipped, also hitting # 1 in the UK, Canada, and Australia. Dion's last French-language studio album of the 1990s, S'il suffisait d'aimer, was also very successful, topping the charts in every major French-speaking country, including France, Switzerland, Belgium Wallonia, and Canada, going diamond in France, selling 1.5 million copies.

By the end of the millennium, Celine had sold more than 100 million L.Ps worldwide, having won any industry awards. Her status as one of the biggest pop divas was further cemented when she was asked to perform on VH1's Divas Live special during 1998, with Aretha Franklin, Gloria Estefan, Shania Twain, and Mariah Carey. Dion also received two of the highest Canadian honours that year: "Officer of the Order of Canada for Outstanding Contribution to the World of Contemporary Music" and "Officer of the National Order of Quebec". She was then inducted into the Canadian Broadcast Hall of Fame in 1999, also being honoured with a star on Canada's Walk of Fame.

Beginning from the mid 1990s, the pop rock influence that was more noticeable in Celine's earlier issues, was replaced by a more mature feel, with the recurring theme of "love" dominating most of her releases, which led to some critics dismissing her music as banal. However, other critics, including Elysa Gardner and Jose F. Promis, praised Dion's voice during this period, describing it as a "technical marvel". Steve Dollar, in his review of These Are Special Times, stated that she was a "vocal Olympian, for whom there ain't no mountain—or scale—high enough".

Following having issued and promoted 13 albums during the 1990s, Celine said that she needed to settle down, announcing on her latest L.P. All the Way... A Decade of Song, that she needed to take a step back from the limelight to enjoy life. Angélil's diagnosis with esophageal cancer also led Dion to take a break, but she was unable to escape media attention.

The National Enquirer published a false story about her during the year 2000, publishing a picture of Celine with her husband, the magazine misquoted her, printing the headline, "Celine — 'I'm Pregnant With Twins!'" She later sued the magazine for more than $20 million, the editors of the Enquirer printing an apology to her with a full retraction in the next issue, donating money to the American Cancer Society in honour of her and her husband. A year later, after undergoing fertility treatments, she gave birth to a son, René-Charles Dion Angélil, on 25th January 2001, in Florida.

After the September 11th terrorist attacks, Celine returned to the music scene, having sung "God Bless America" during the televised benefit concert, America: A Tribute to Heroes. Chuck Taylor of Billboard wrote, "the performance ... brings to mind what has made her one of the most celebrated vocalists of our time: the ability to render emotion that shakes the soul. Affecting, meaningful, and filled with grace, this is a musical reflection to share with all of us still searching for ways to cope." Dion performed the song again in 2003, during pregame festivities for Super Bowl XXXVII in San Diego. She published her autobiography, My Story, My Dream in December 2001, chronicling her rags-to-riches story.

Celine ended her 3-year hiatus from the music industry with the album A New Day Has Come, released during March 2002. The L.P. was her most personal yet, with songs focusing on her having become a mother and maturing as a woman, including, "A New Day Has Come", and "Goodbye's (The Saddest Word)".

Dion stated: "Becoming a mother makes you a grown-up. A New Day Has Come, for Rene, for me, its the baby. It has everything to do with the baby ... That song "A New Day Has Come" represents very well the mood I'm feeling right now. It represents the whole album." A New Day Has Come debuted at the top of the charts in over 17 countries, including the UK and Canada. In the US, the L.P. entered the Billboard 200 at the top, with first-week sales of 527,000 copies, her first No. 1 debut on the chart, as well as the highest first sales week of her career in the US. It was later certified 3× Platinum in the US, and 6× Platinum in Canada.

Despite the album being yet another big seller, critical reviews described it as "forgettable," stating that the lyrics were "lifeless". Both Rob Sheffield of Rolling Stone magazine, and Ken Tucker of Entertainment Weekly, said that Celine's music hadn't developed much during her break, rating her material as trite and mediocre. Sal Cinquemani of Slant Magazine dismissed the

L.P. as "a lengthy collection of drippy, gooey, pop fluffer-nutter".

The first single off the album, A New Day Has Come made No.22 on the Billboard Hot 100 charts, being an airplay-only issue. However, on the Hot Adult Contemporary Tracks chart, the song spent 21 successive weeks at No. 1, breaking the record for the longest time at the top. The previous record holders were Phil Collins' You'll Be in My Heart and Dion's own Because You Loved Me, both of which spent 19 weeks at No. 1. Celine performed for many benefit concerts during 2002, including her 2nd appearance on VH1 Divas Live, a concert to benefit the VH1 Save The Music Foundation, alongside Cher, Anastacia, Dixie Chicks, Mary J. Blige, Whitney Houston, Cyndi Lauper, Shakira, and Stevie Nicks.

Dion issued One Heart (2003), a L.P. which represented her appreciation for life, in conjunction with an endorsement deal with Chrysler. The album largely comprised pop and dance music—a change from the soaring, melodramatic ballads, for which Celine had become known. Although the L.P. was moderately successful, One Heart got mixed reviews, words including "predictable" and "banal" having been used to describe it. A cover of the Cyndi Lauper hit "I Drove All Night" of 1989, released to launch her ad campaign with Chrysler, incorporated elements of dance-pop and rock 'n' roll. The advertising deal was criticised, with some stating that Dion was trying to cater to her sponsors.

Following One Heart, she issued her next English-language studio album, Miracle (2004), a multimedia project conceived by Celine and Australian photographer Anne Geddes, which had a theme centring on babies and motherhood. The L.P. was filled with lullabies and other songs of maternal love and inspiration, including covers of Louis Armstrong's "What a Wonderful World" and John Lennon's "Beautiful Boy".

The reviews for Miracle were mixed, Stephen Thomas Erlewine of Allmusic.com giving the album 3 of out 5 stars, stating, "The worst you can say about the record is that there are no surprises, but the audience for this record doesn't want surprises; they want comfort, whether it arrives in polished music or artsy photos of newborns, and Miracle provides both, which makes it appealing for those expectant or new mothers in Dion's audience."

Chuck Taylor of Billboard magazine wrote that the single "Beautiful Boy" was "an unexpected gem", having called Celine "a timeless, enormously versatile artist", but Chuck Arnold of People Magazine labelled the album as excessively sentimental, while Nancy Miller of Entertainment Weekly believed that "the whole earth-mama act is just opportunism, reborn". Miracle debuted at No. 4 on the Billboard 200 chart, while topping the Canadian charts, later being certified platinum by the RIAA.

The francophone album 1 fille & 4 types (1 Girl & 4 Guys), released during October 2003, sold better than her previous 2 issues, as Dion tried to distance herself from the "diva" image. She recruited Jean-Jacques Goldman, Gildas Arzel, Eric Benzi, and Jacques Veneruso, with whom she'd previously worked on two of her best-selling French L.Ps S'il suffisait d'aimer and D'eux.

Labeled "the album of pleasure" by Celine, the cover showed her in a simple, relaxed manner, contrasting with the choreographed poses usually found on her L.P. covers. The album sold well in France, Canada, and Belgium, where it topped the charts, also entering the French charts at No. 1, later being certified 2× platinum after selling over 700,000 copies. Critic Stephen Erlewine of AllMusic wrote that Dion's vocals were "back at the top of their game" and that she was "getting back to pop basics and performing at a level unheard for a while".

Though her latest L.Ps were successful, they didn't have the same magnitude of sales or the good reception of her previous discs. Her songs received less airplay as radio became less receptive to balladeers including Celine, Mariah Carey, and Whitney Houston, being focused on more up-tempo, Urban/Hip-hop songs.

Dion had sold over 175 million albums worldwide by 2004, having received the Chopard Diamond Award from the World Music Awards for her achievements, their website stating that the award was "not presented every year" an artist only becoming eligible to receive it by selling "over 100 million albums during their career".

Celine announced a 3-year, 600-show contract to appear 5 nights / week in an entertainment extravaganza, A New Day..., at The Colosseum at Caesars Palace, Las Vegas during early 2002. The move was generally seen as risky, but journalist Miriam Nunzio wrote that it was "one of the smartest business decisions in years by any major recording artist".

Dion conceived the show after seeing O by Franco Dragone during her break from recording, it having begun on 25th March 2003, in a 4,000-seat arena specifically designed for her show, modelled on the Roman Colosseum. Many stars attended the opening night, including Dick Clark, Alan Thicke, Kathy Griffin, Lance Bass, and Justin Timberlake, who hosted the TV special.

The show, directed by Dragone, having been choreographed by the renowned Mia Michaels, was a combination of dance, music, and visual effects. It included Celine performing her biggest hits against an array of dancers and special effects. Reviewer Mike Weatherford felt that at first Dion wasn't as relaxed as she should've been, while at times it was hard to make out the singer among the excessive stage ornamentation and dancers. However, he observed that the show had become more enjoyable over the course of its run, because of her improved stage-presence and simplified costumes.

The show was well-received by audiences, it having routinely sold out until its end in late 2007, despite complaints of expensive ticket prices, which averaged $135.33. Pollstar stated that Celine sold 322,000 tickets, grossing US$43.9 million in the first half of 2005, having sold out 315 out of 384 shows by July 2005. By the end of that year she grossed more than US$76 million, being 6th on Billboard's Money Makers list for 2005.

A New Day... was also the 6th biggest-selling tour in the US the following year, so her contract was extended into 2007 for an undisclosed sum. On 5th January that year it was announced that the show would end on 15th December 2007, with tickets for the period after October having gone on sale from 1st March. Billboard stated that, A New Day... was the most successful residency of all time, grossing over US$385 million, having drawing nearly 3 million people to 717 shows. The Live in Las Vegas: A New Day... DVD was released on 10th December 2007 in Europe then the following day in North America.

Dion issued the French-language L.P. D'elles (About Them) on 21st May 2007, which debuted at the top of the Canadian album charts, selling 72,200 copies in its first week. It was her 10th chart-topping L.P. in the SoundScan era, her 8th to enter the charts at # 1, having also topped the charts in France and Belgium. In Canada, the album was later certified 2× platinum, having shipped half a million units worldwide within its first month.

Its lead single "Et s'il n'en restait qu'une (je serais celle-là)" ("And If There Was Only One Woman Left (I Would Be That One)") had entered the French singles chart at the top a month earlier. Later that same year, Celine issued the English L.P. Taking Chances on 12th November 2007 in Europe, delayed by a day in North America. Her first English studio album since One Heart in 2003, it featured pop, R&B, and rock inspired music.

Dion collaborated with John Shanks and ex-Evanescence guitarist Ben Moody on the L.P., as well as Kristian Lundin, Peer Åström, Linda Perry, Japanese singer Yuna Ito, and R&B singer-songwriter Ne-Yo. Celine stated, "I think this album represents a positive evolution in my career ... I'm feeling strong, maybe a little gutsier than in the past, and just as passionate about music and life as I ever was." She launched her year-long worldwide Taking Chances Tour on 14th February 2008, in South Africa, performing 132 dates in stadiums and arenas across 5 continents.

The Taking Chances Tour was a great success in the US, topping the Billboard Boxscore, having sold out every concert in the US and Canada. Dion appeared on Idol Gives Back for the 2nd consecutive year then was nominated for 6 Juno Awards in 2008, on top of her 53 previous nominations, an all-time record.

Celine's nominations included Artist of the Year, Pop Album of the Year for Taking Chances, Francophone Album of the Year for

D'elles and Album of the Year for both. The following year, she was nominated for 3 Juno Awards, including the Fan Choice Award, Song of the Year for Taking Chances, and Music DVD of the Year for Live in Las Vegas — A New Day...

Dion presented a free outdoor concert, mostly in French, on the Plains of Abraham, in Québec City, Canada on 22nd August 2008, for the 400th anniversary of Québec City, the celebration attracting c. 490,000 people. The concert, called Céline sur les Plaines, was released on DVD on 11th November that year in Québec, before being issued on 20th May 2009, in France. A comprehensive English-language greatest hits L.P., My Love: Essential Collection was released worldwide during late October 2008.

Dion was named the 20th best-selling artist of the decade and the 2nd-best-selling female artist of the decade in the US during May 2009, having sold an estimated 17.57 million copies of her albums there since the year 2000. Forbes reported the following month that she'd earned $100 million during 2008. Pollstar announced during December 2009 that Céline was the best-selling solo touring act of the decade and the 2nd-best-selling touring act of the decade, behind only the Dave Matthews Band. She grossed $522.2 million during the decade, a large part of that sum coming from her 5-year residency at Caesars Palace.

Dion released a documentary film about her Taking Chances Tour into cinemas on 17th February 2010, titled, Celine: Through the Eyes of the World. The documentary featured behind-the-scenes footage of her both onstage and offstage, along with footage of Dion with her family as they travelled the world with her. The distributor was the Sony Pictures subsidiary, Hot Ticket. The film was later issued on Blu-ray and DVD on 4th

May 2010, along with the CD/DVD, Taking Chances World Tour: The Concert. At the 52nd Grammy Awards in February 2010, Celine joined Carrie Underwood, Usher, Jennifer Hudson, and Smokey Robinson to perform "Earth Song" during a 3-D Michael Jackson tribute.

The Los Angeles Times presented its annual list of the top 10 biggest earners of the year during January 2010, revealing that Dion had taken the top spot for the entire decade, with $US747.9 million in total income from 2000–2009, the largest part having come from ticket sales, of $522.2 million. Celine was also named "Artist of the Decade" in her native Canadian province of Québec, as announced by the Montréal-based newspaper, Le Journal de Québec in 2009 December, a public online survey having asked respondents to vote for whom they believed most deserved the accolade.

Dion was named the most popular artist in the US in a May 2010 Harris Poll, ahead of U2, Elvis Presley, and The Beatles, while factoring in gender, political affiliations, geographic region of residence, and income. Celine was the most popular musician amongst females, as well as among all Democrats, those who lived in the eastern US, southern US, and those who had incomes of between US$35k and US$74.9k.

She released the single "Voler", during September 2010, a duet with French singer Michel Sardou, the song later being included on Sardou's L.P. The following month it was announced that Dion had written and composed a new song for Canadian singer, Marc Dupré entitled "Entre deux mondes".

Dion announced in February 2010 that she'd be returning to Caesars Palace in Las Vegas for Celine, a 3-year residency of 70 shows / year, starting on 15th March 2011. She stated that the show would feature, "all the songs from my repertoire that people want to hear" also including a selection of music from classic Hollywood movies.

To promote her return to Las Vegas, Dion featured on The Oprah Winfrey Show on 21st February, during the show's final season, her record 27th appearance. She also performed at the 83rd Academy Awards for a record 6th time, where she sang the song "Smile", as part of the ceremony's "In Memoriam" part. Celine appeared on the MDA Labor Telethon Event on 4th September, presenting a prerecorded performance of "Open Arms" from her new Las Vegas show. She then made an appearance at the free concert of world-famous tenor, Andrea Bocelli, in Central Park in New York on 15th September. The 14th perfume from her Celine Dion Parfums Collection was issued that month, named "Signature".

The OWN Network premiered a documentary on her life on 1st October 2011, detailing the months before, during and after her pregnancy, to the makings of her new Las Vegas Show, titled, "Celine: 3 Boys and a New Show", which became the 2nd highest rated show on TV OWN Canada. FlightNetwork.com conducted a poll that month, asking 780 people which celebrity they'd most like to sit next to on an airplane, Dion being their favourite, with 23.7% of the vote. She performed at the 16th Jazz and Blues Festival in Jamaica during 2012.

Sony Music Entertainment released The Best of Celine Dion & David Foster in Asia during October that year, having begun recording songs for her next English and French albums during

April and May 2012. The French-language L.P., Sans attendre was issued on 2nd November, becoming a hit in all French-speaking territories, being particularly big in France, where it went diamond.

The English-language album was postponed to 1st November 2013, being titled Loved Me Back to Life, featuring collaborations with a leading team of songwriters and producers, including duets with Ne-Yo and Stevie Wonder. The lead single, "Loved Me Back to Life" had been released on 3rd September that year. Celine embarked on the Sans attendre Tour during November 2013, performing in Belgium and France.

"Breakaway", "Incredible" and "Water and a Flame" were chosen as the following singles, the music video for "Incredible" being uploaded onto her official Vevo channel in early June 2014. Dion had issued a 3-disc set (2CD/DVD and 2CD/Blu-ray) on 16th May that year, titled Céline une seule fois / Live 2013, which entered the top 10 on the album charts in France, Canada and Belgium Wallonia.

Dion announced the indefinite postponement of all her show business activities on 13th August 2014, including her concert residency at Caesars Palace in Las Vegas, and the cancellation of her Asia Tour, because of the decline in her husband's health after he underwent the removal of a cancerous tumor during December 2013. However, Céline announced on 20th March 2015 that she'd be returning to The Colosseum at Caesars Palace in late August that year, before cancelling the remainder of her January 2016 performances on 14th of that month, due to both her husband's and brother's deaths from cancer. Dion resumed her residency on 23rd February to a sold-out crowd and rave reviews.

Céline had announced on social media during October 2015 that she'd begun working on a new French L.P., posting a photo by the side of Algerian singer Zaho, her French single, "Encore un soir", being released on 24th May 2016. She'd issued a cover of Queen's song "The Show Must Go On", on 20th May, featuring Lindsey Stirling on violin, which she performed at the Billboard Music Awards on 22nd May, where she received the Billboard Icon Award, presented to her by her son, René-Charles Angélil, in recognition of her career, spanning over 3 decades.

Dion's new French album, Encore un soir, was released on 26th August 2016, featuring 15 tracks performed in French, having chosen those with uplifting lyrics. The record topped the charts in France, Canada, Belgium and Switzerland, being certified Diamond in France, 2× Platinum in Canada and Platinum in Belgium and Switzerland, having sold over 1.5 million copies worldwide.

Céline toured Europe and Canada during 2016 and 2017, with two sold-out concert tours. She released "Recovering" on 9th September 2016, a song written for Dion by Pink after her husband René Angélil died. Céline also recorded "How Does a Moment Last Forever" for the Beauty and the Beast: Original Motion Picture Soundtrack, issued during March 2017. Her compilation, Un peu de nous topped the charts in France in July and August that year.

Dion released the single "Ashes" from the film Deadpool 2 on 3rd May 2018, the remix version of the song topping the US Dance Club Songs chart during July that year. From June to August 2018, she toured the Asia-Pacific region, having grossed $56.5 million from 22 shows. She announced the end of her Las Vegas residency Celine on 24th September, with the final date set for 8th June 2019, having started working on a new English L.P. She performed "A Change Is Gonna Come" during January 2019, at the "Aretha! A Grammy Celebration for the Queen of Soul," Franklin's tribute concert, to be broadcast in March.

Dion has cited her idols as Aretha Franklin, Charles Aznavour, Michael Jackson, Carole King, Anne Murray, Barbra Streisand, and the Bee Gees, all of whom she has collaborated with. Celine's music has been influenced by many genres, including pop, rock, gospel, R&B, and soul, with her lyrics having focused on themes including poverty, world hunger, and spirituality, with an emphasis on love and romance. After the birth of her first child, her work increasingly focused on maternal love.

Dion's music has frequently been disparaged by the critics, who've stated that she's often retreated behind pop and soul conventions, being over sentimental. Keith Harris of Rolling Stone magazine wrote that Celine's "sentimentality is bombastic and defiant, rather than demure and retiring ... she stands at the end of the chain of drastic devolution that goes Aretha–Whitney–Mariah. Far from being an aberration, Dion actually stands as a symbol of a certain kind of pop sensibility—bigger is better, too much is never enough, and the riper the emotion the more true." In contrast her francophone issues have tended to be deeper and more varied than her English releases, having been recieved with more credibility by the critics.

They've stated that Celine's involvement with the production aspects of her music is fundamentally lacking, which has led to her work being overproduced and impersonal. However, coming from a family in which all of her siblings were musicians, she dabbled in learning how to play instruments including piano and guitar, having practised with a Fender Stratocaster during the recording sessions of her album, Falling into You.

Dion has contributed to writing a handful of her English and French songs, as well as writing a few songs for other artists including Marc Dupre. As her career progressed, Celine started taking charge in the production of her L.Ps. She expressed disapproval of her first English album, which Dion recorded before she had a firm command of the English language, which could've been avoided if she'd had more creative input.

By the time she released her 2nd English album Celine Dion, she'd taken more control over the production and recording process, hoping to dispel earlier criticisms. She stated, "On the 2nd album I said, 'Well, I have the choice to be afraid one more time and not be 100% happy, or not be afraid and be part of this album.' This is my album." Along with her contributions to some of her early French L.Ps, Celine wrote a few of the songs on Let's Talk About Love (1997) and These Are Special Times (1998).

She has often been the subject of media ridicule and parody, frequently having been impersonated on shows including MADtv, Saturday Night Live, South Park, Royal Canadian Air Farce, and This Hour Has 22 Minutes, for her strong accent and on-stage gesticulations. However, Dion's stated that she's unaffected by the comments, being flattered that people take the time to impersonate her.

Celine invited Ana Gasteyer, who parodied her on SNL, to appear on stage during one of her performances in New York. While she's rarely politically outspoken, following the Hurricane Katrina disaster of 2005, Dion appeared on Larry King Live to tearfully criticize the US government's slow response to aiding victims of the hurricane:

"There's people still there waiting to be rescued. To me that's not acceptable ... How can it be so easy to send planes into another country to kill everybody in a second and destroy lives. We need to serve our country." Afterwards she stated, "When I do interviews with Larry King or the big TV shows like that, they put you on the spot, which is very difficult. I do have an opinion, but I'm a singer. I'm not a politician."

Celine is often regarded as one of pop music's most influential voices, Linda Lister in Divafication: The Deification of Modern Female Pop Stars, describing her as a reigning "Queen of Pop" for her influence over the record industry during the 1990s, alongside other female singers, including Whitney Houston and Mariah Carey. In a countdown of the "22 Greatest Voices in Music" by Blender Magazine and MTV, she was placed 9th (6th highest female), having also ranked 4th in Cover Magazine's list of "The 100 Outstanding Pop Vocalists". Dion is often compared to Mariah Carey and Whitney Houston for her vocal style and to her idol, Barbra Streisand, for her voice.

Celine has a 3-octave range, from B2 to E♭6, having once stated that she's a mezzo-soprano but attempts to adapt classical voice types to other forms of singing have been controversial. Without making a classification, maestro Kent Nagano remarked, "All you just sang was full lyric soprano", after Dion auditioned with two solos from Carmen, wanting to know if she could sing opera. Her timbre has been described as "thin, slightly nasal," with a "raspy" lower register and "bell glass-like high notes".

Celine is often praised for her technical virtuosity, Jim Santella of The Buffalo News having written "Like an iron fist in a velvet glove, the power of Celine Dion's voice is cloaked in a silky vibrato that betrays the intensity of her vocal commitment." Jeff Miers, also of The Buffalo News, said of Dion "Her singing voice is absolutely extra-human. She hits notes in full voice, with a controlled vibrato and an incredible conception of pitch, like she's shucking an ear of corn"

Stephen Holden of The New York Times stated that Dion has "a good-sized arsenal of technical skills. She can deliver tricky melismas, produce expressive vocal catches and sustain long notes, without the tiniest wavering of pitch, and as her duets ... have shown, she is a reliable harmony voice." In an interview with Libération, Jean-Jacques Goldman observed that she has "no problem of accuracy or tempo".

Kent Nagano, maestro of the Munich Symphony Orchestra, said that Celine is "a musician who has a good ear, a refinement, and a degree of perfection that is enviable". Charles Alexander of Time stated that her "voice glides effortlessly from deep whispers to dead-on high notes, a sweet siren that combines force with grace."

In her French repertoire, Dion adorns her vocals with more nuances and expressiveness, with the emotional intensity being "more tender and intimate". Luc Plamondon, a French singer-songwriter who's worked closely with Celine believes that there are 3 chanteuses (stylistically) that she uses: the Québécois, the French, and the American. Her eponymous L.P. was promoted with the slogan "Remember the name because you'll never forget the voice."

Dion is regarded as one of pop music's most influential voices, her music and vocal style having been said to shape how most modern female pop vocalists sing, alongside that of Mariah Carey and Whitney Houston. These 3 singers have been widely credited with reviving the power ballad, by doing so reshaping the adult contemporary radio format, making it one of the most popular formats of the 1990s and early 2000s.

Producer, musician, and former American Idol judge Randy Jackson stated that Celine, Mariah Carey, and Whitney Houston are the voices of the modern era. Carl Wilson, music critic and biographer of Dion, observed that her "fame and influence is also renewed and expressed regularly these days by American Idol, the largest mass musical phenomenon of the past decade, where Celine's stood solidly in its pantheon of singers for young people to emulate". Numerous contestants on the many televised talent competitions that have arisen since the turn of the millennium have emulated Dion, Houston and Carey, citing them as idols.

Many artists have either mentioned Celine as a major influence or as one of their favourite singers including: Britney Spears, Rihanna, Christina Aguilera, Frank Ocean, Adele, Josh Groban, Delta Goodrem, Jordin Sparks, Charice, Leona Lewis, Jessie J, Jojo, Lea Michele, Jennifer Hudson, Ariana Grande, Regine Velasquez, Taylor Swift, Vanessa Hudgens, The Canadian Tenors, Faith Hill, Katy Perry, Sevyn Streeter and Kelly Clarkson, among many others. Country singer Martina McBride has been widely labeled by the press as the Celine Dion of Country music.

Numerous artists have also praised Dion's voice, singing ability or expressed an interest in working with her including Beyoncé, Carlos Santana, Elton John, OneRepublic, Coldplay, Sharon

Osbourne, Nicole Scherzinger, Ne-Yo, Carole King, Barbra Streisand, Luciano Pavarotti, Bee Gees, Sir George Martin, Justin Bieber, Jean-Jacques Goldman, and Cher.

Justin Timbaland stated, "Celine has such a beautiful, mesmerizing voice. She's so talented. I think we could create something that is a classic like she is already." Josh Groban said "She's a powerhouse. In this day and age, when more and more studio-produced, tiny-tiny voices are being rewarded ... she has this extraordinary instrument."

Diane Warren believed that "Celine is the best singer by far of her generation," an opinion shared by Quincy Jones, Tommy Mottola, and David Foster. Shania Twain and Jennifer Lopez have praised her dynamic stage presence, with the latter saying on American Idol: "Celine gets on stage, she owns the stage, she runs all over that stage, she stops that stage."

Dion is credited for introducing French music to many non-francophone countries around the globe. Her albums D'eux and S'il suffisait d'aimer remain the best selling French L.Ps in history, having unprecedented success in non-Francophone markets including the UK, Poland, Netherlands, Portugal, Greece, Austria, Japan, and New Zealand.

RFI Musique stated that she "has done her bit for French music over the years, assuring the success of French songs which would probably never have got beyond Francophone borders without her ... Without Celine, French record sales would be dramatically lower!" She received the Legion of Honour from Nicolas Sarkozy during 2008, who praised Dion: "France thanks you because your talent and success have contributed to the influence of the French language outside our borders".

Celine has also been credited for both revitalizing and revolutionizing the entertainment scene in Las Vegas, with the great successes of her residencies there. Dion re-popularized the Las Vegas "residency" as a desirable way for top artists to perform for their fans, fellow established icons including Elton John, Bette Midler, Rod Stewart, Cher, and Shania Twain having followed suit over the years.

Gary Bongiovanni, president and editor-in-chief of Pollstar stated "Celine redefined what artists can do in Las Vegas, helping to make it arguably the busiest entertainment city in the world." Britney Spears announced a Vegas residency during 2013, Kurt Melien, vice-president of entertainment at Caesar's Palace saying: "Celine was a pioneer without question ... 20 years ago, we couldn't have got someone of the stature of Britney Spears to appear in Vegas. Stars like her would never have considered it if Celine hadn't paved the way. She changed the face of modern Vegas."

Regarding her financial impact on Las Vegas, Stephen Brown, director of the Centre for Business and Economic Research in Las Vegas, said "People will come to the city just for her, they will spend money and as a consequence, she has an outsized impact on the economy. Bigger than Elvis, Sinatra and Liberace put together? Definitely." Estimates indicated that Dion's show would've created up to 7,000 indirect jobs, with c. $114 million worth of new economic activity in each of the 3 years for which she'd been contracted.

The Canadian comedy music group, The Arrogant Worms, issued an album titled Dirt in 1999, which included a song named "Celine Dion", about the singer's stalker-like affection for her. That year Celine received a star on Canada's Walk of Fame, being inducted into the Canadian Broadcast Hall of Fame, a star on the Hollywood Walk of Fame following during January 2004, which she dedicated to her father, who'd died the previous month. Dion was ranked at No. 10 on VH1's list of "50 Greatest Women of the Video Era" in May 2003 and at No. 64 on their list of the "200 Greatest Pop Culture Icons of All Time". Her L.P. Falling Into You has been put on the Rock and Roll Hall of Fame's Definitive 200 list.

"My Heart Will Go On" was included in the Recording Industry Association of America and the National Endowment for the Arts list of Songs of the Century. Celine was ranked by Forbes as the 5th richest woman in entertainment during 2007, with an estimated net worth of US$250 million, although the ranking omitted non-working or retired celebrities. She received an honorary doctorate in music from the Université Laval in Quebec City during August 2008.

Dion was named a Goodwill Ambassador in October 2010, a program created by the UN in 1999, sharing the accolade with Oscar-winner Susan Sarandon, having also received several state decorations. Celine was awarded a Society of Singers Lifetime Achievement Award during 2004 then was given France's highest award, the Légion d'honneur, by President Nicolas Sarkozy in May 2008. Dion was awarded the highest rank of the Order of Canada on 26th July 2013, the Companion of the Order of Canada, by the Governor General of Canada, the investiture ceremony being held at Citadelle of Quebec, the same year she was inducted into the Gaming Hall of Fame.

Les Productions Feeling Inc., also known as Feeling Inc. or just Feeling, is an artist management company based in Laval, Québec, Canada, which was owned by Celine and her husband and manager, Rene Angélil. Dion owned Le Mirage Golf Club and Schwartz's Restaurant with her husband, having also opened a popular night club called Pure, located at Caesars Palace, in association with Andre Agassi, Steffi Graf and Shaquille O'Neal.

Celine became an entrepreneur with the establishment of her franchise restaurant Nickels during 1990, having since divested her interests in the chain, no longer being affiliated with Nickels, as of 1997. Dion signed a deal with Coty, Inc. to release Celine Dion Parfums during 2003, her latest fragrance, Signature, coming out in September 2011, supported by an ad campaign by New York agency Kraftworks NYC.

Since its inception, Celine Dion Parfums has grossed over $850 million in retail sales. Air Canada hired Celine during October 2004, as part of their promotional campaign to unveil new service products and an updated livery. "You and I", the theme song sung by Dion, was written by advertising executives working for Air Canada.

Celine has actively supported many charity organizations, worldwide, having promoted the Canadian Cystic Fibrosis Foundation (CCFF) since 1982, becoming the foundation's National Celebrity Patron inv 1993. She has an emotional attachment to the foundation; her niece Karine having succumbed to the disease in Dion's arms at the age of 16.

Celine joined a number of other celebrities, athletes, and politicians, including Josh Groban and Yolanda Adams in 2003, to support "World Children's Day", a global fundraising effort sponsored by McDonald's, which raised money from more than 100 nations, benefiting orphanages and children's health organizations.

Dion has also been a major supporter of the T. J. Martell Foundation, the Diana Princess of Wales Memorial Fund, and many health and educational campaigns. She donated $1 million to the victims of Hurricane Katrina, having held a fund-raising event for the victims of the 2004 Asian tsunami, which raised more than $1 million. Following the Sichuan earthquake of 2008, Celine donated $100,000 to China Children & Teenagers' Fund, sending a letter showing her sympathy and support.

Dion was involved with the Québec gay community from 2004, alongside her husband René Angelil, supporting the publication of health and HIV prevention materials in Gay Globe Magazine, owned by journalist Roger-Luc Chayer. She's also a member of Canadian charity Artists Against Racism. Celine launched a gender-neutral clothing line for kids, Celinununu, during November 2018.

Dion lives in Henderson, Nevada. She first met her husband and manager, René Angélil, in 1980, when she was 12 and he was 38, after her brother, Michel Dondalinger Dion, sent him a demonstration recording of "Ce n'était qu'un rêve" ("It Was Only a Dream/Nothing But A Dream"), a song that she, her mother, the former Thérèse Tanguay, and her brother Jacques Dion had jointly written and composed. Celine and Angélil began a relationship during 1987, became engaged in 1991 then married on 17th December 1994, at Notre-Dame Basilica in Montreal, Quebec. Dion and Angélil renewed their wedding vows in Las Vegas on 5th January 2000.

Celine had two small operations at a fertility clinic in New York during May 2000 to improve her chances of conceiving, after deciding to use in-vitro fertilization because of years of failed attempts to conceive. Their first son, René-Charles Angélil, was born on 25th January 2001. Angélil announced that Dion was 14 weeks pregnant with twins during May 2010, after a 6th treatment of in-vitro fertilization.

Celine gave birth to healthy fraternal twins by Caesarean section on Saturday, 23rd October 2010, at 11:11 and 11:12 am respectively, at St. Mary's Medical Center in West Palm Beach, Florida. The twins were named Eddy, after Dion's favourite French songwriter, Eddy Marnay, who'd also produced her first 5 albums, and Nelson, after former South African President Nelson Mandela. She appeared with her newborn sons on the cover of the 9th December 2010 issue of the Canadian edition of Hello! magazine.

Angélil died from complications of cancer on 14th January 2016. Two days later her brother Daniel also died of cancer, aged 59. Celine's management team announced on 22nd March 2018 that she'd been dealing with hearing irregularities for the previous 12–18 months due to Patulous Eustachian tube, so would be undergoing a minimally invasive surgical procedure to correct the problem, after ear-drop medications appeared to be no longer working.

Discography

French-language studio albums

La voix du bon Dieu (1981)

Céline Dion chante Noël (1981)

Tellement j'ai d'amour... (1982)

Les chemins de ma maison (1983)

Chants et contes de Noël (1983)

Mélanie (1984)

C'est pour toi (1985)

Incognito (1987)

Dion chante Plamondon (1991)

D'eux (1995)

S'il suffisait d'aimer (1998)

1 fille & 4 types (2003)

D'elles (2007)

Sans attendre (2012)

Encore un soir (2016)

English-language studio albums

Unison (1990)

Celine Dion (1992)

The Colour of My Love (1993)

Falling into You (1996)

Let's Talk About Love (1997)

These Are Special Times (1998)

A New Day Has Come (2002)

One Heart (2003)

Miracle (2004)

Taking Chances (2007)

Loved Me Back to Life (2013)

Concert tours and residencies

Year	Title	Releases
1985	Céline Dion en concert	Céline Dion en concert
1988	Incognito tournée	N/A
1990–1991	Unison Tour	Unison
1992–1993	Celine Dion in Concert	N/A

1994–1995   The Colour of My Love Tour   The Colour of My Love Concert

À l'Olympia

1995–1996   D'eux Tour   Live à Paris (video)

Live à Paris

1996–1997   Falling into You: Around the World   Live in Memphis

1998–1999   Let's Talk About Love World Tour   Au cœur du stade (video)

Au cœur du stade

2003–2007   A New Day...   Live in Las Vegas: A New Day...

A New Day... Live in Las Vegas

2008–2009   Taking Chances World Tour   Céline sur les Plaines

Celine: Through the Eyes of the World

Taking Chances World Tour: The Concert

2011–2019   Celine

2013   Tournée Européenne 2013   Céline une seule fois / Live 2013

2014   Asia Tour (cancelled)   N/A

2016   Summer Tour 2016

2017   Celine Dion Live 2017

2018   Celine Dion Live 2018

Filmography

Touched by an Angel

The Nanny

All My Children

La fureur de Céline

Des fleurs sur la neige

Quest for Camelot as Juliana (singing voice)

Céline sur les Plaines

Celine: Through the Eyes of the World

Sur la piste du Marsupilami

Hell's Kitchen

Muppets Most Wanted

Bibliography

Michaels, Sean (22 July 2011). "Celine Dion shuts down parody website". The Guardian. London.

Beaulne, Jean (2004). René Angélil: the making of Céline Dion : the unauthorized biography. Dundurn Group. ISBN 978-1-55002-489-0.

Bogdanov, Vladimir; Woodstra; Erlewine (2001). Allmusic:The Definitive Guide to Popular Music. Backbeat Books. ISBN 978-0-87930-627-4.

Céline Dion. Artist direct.

"Celine Dion". Contemporary Musicians, Volume 25. Gale Group, 1999.

"Celine Dion". Newsmakers 1995, Issue 4. Gale Research, 1995.

Céline Dion Rock on the Net.

Céline Dion The Canadian Encyclopedia.

Céline Dion provided by VH1.com

Dion extends long Las Vegas stint bbc news. com.

Durchholz, Daniel. Review: One Heart. St. Louis Post-Dispatch. St. Louis, Mo.: 24 April 2003. p. F.3

Germain, Georges-Hébert (1998). Céline: The Authorized Biography. Dundurn Press. ISBN 978-1-55002-318-3.

Glatzer, Jenna (2005). Céline Dion: For Keeps. Becker & Mayer Ltd. ISBN 978-0-7407-5559-0.

The 100 Outstanding Pop Vocalist covemagazine.com

Joel Whitburn Presents the Billboard Hot 100 Charts: The Nineties (ISBN 0-89820-137-3)

Further reading

Beauregard, Sylvain (2002). Passion Celine Dion the Book: The Ultimate Guide for the Fan. Trafford Pub. ISBN 978-1-55369-212-6. Archived from the original on 7 February 2016.

Dion, Céline (2001). Céline Dion: My Story, My Dream. Avon. ISBN 978-0-380-81905-8.

Geddes, Anne; Céline Dion (2004). Miracle: a celebration of new life. Andrews McMeel Pub. ISBN 978-0-7407-4696-3. Archived from the original on 3 June 2016.

Wilson, Carl (2007). Let's Talk About Love: A Journey to the End of Taste. Continuum. ISBN 978-0-8264-2788-5.

47

64

Lightning Source UK Ltd.
Milton Keynes UK
UKHW051308171219
355484UK00015B/391/P